Martin Luther King Jr.

Wendy Conklin, M.A.

Publishing Credits

Historical Consultant
Shannon C. McCutchen

Editor
Torrey Maloof

Editorial Director
Emily R. Smith, M.A.Ed.

Editor-in-Chief
Sharon Coan, M.S.Ed.

Creative Director
Lee Aucoin

Illustration Manager
Timothy J. Bradley

Publisher
Rachelle Cracchiolo, M.S.Ed.

Teacher Created Materials
5301 Oceanus Drive
Huntington Beach, CA 92649-1030
http://www.tcmpub.com

ISBN 978-0-7439-0671-5

Printed by: 590835
Printed in: China

Table of Contents

The Dreamer

If ever there was a dreamer, it was Martin Luther King Jr. When he was just a little kid, he told his mother he was going to turn this world upside down. There is no denying that this first dream came true. At that age, he had no idea he would fight his nation's second civil war. It is certain that King had many more dreams, but there was one that stood out from the rest. He said, "I have a dream that my four little children will one day live in a nation where they will not be judged by the color of their skin but by the content of their character."

This movie theater had two entrances, one for white people and one for African Americans. African Americans had to enter upstairs through a separate door.

King was a very gifted speaker. His words motivated people across the country.

King grew up during a very difficult time in the South. The South had laws that kept races separate from one another. African Americans and whites could not go to the same restaurants or drink from the same fountains. This treatment is called **segregation** (seg-rih-GAY-shuhn).

People in the South called these laws, the Jim Crow laws. This referred to a character from the 1800s. At that time, some white actors painted their faces black. Then they put on shows for entertainment. Jim Crow was a famous character from those shows. This character made African Americans look silly.

A Famous Court Case

In 1892, a man named Homer Plessy wanted to test the Fourteenth Amendment. This amendment says that all men have equal protection under the law. In other words, all men should be treated equally.

Seven out of eight of Plessy's great-grandparents were white. But laws in the South said that because Plessy had African American relatives, he was not a white man. When Plessy sat in the part of the train for white people, the police arrested him.

Plessy's case went to the United States Supreme Court. They ruled that as long as both African Americans and whites had seating on trains, then it was okay that they had to sit separately. This was called "separate but equal." In the end, the case of *Plessy v. Ferguson* made the Jim Crow laws **legal**.

Booker T. Washington

Two Leaders

The African American community was not always united. Booker T. Washington was the son of a white man and a slave. He thought that African Americans should make the best of their lives. He felt African Americans could advance if they worked hard and educated themselves. His school, the Tuskegee Institute, taught African Americans crafts and trades so they could get better jobs.

W. E. B. Du Bois (doo-BOZ) did not like Washington's idea of waiting for "separate but equal" to end. He wanted *everything* to be equal for African Americans immediately. This is what led to the formation of the NAACP.

The Father Who Was an Activist

King's father, Reverend Martin Luther King Sr., was the minister of a church in Atlanta, Georgia. He joined the National Association for the Advancement of Colored People (NAACP). This group felt that African Americans should be treated the same as white people. Getting rid of the Jim Crow laws was a goal of the NAACP. So, the group's lawyers went to court. When a judge threw out one of the laws, **segregationists** (seg-rih-GAY-shuhn-istz) passed new Jim Crow laws. It seemed as if the NAACP made very little progress.

Reverend King was an **activist**. He led a march to get African Americans to vote. He also argued that Atlanta should pay African American teachers the same as white teachers. Reverend King stood up for what he believed. He taught his son to do the same.

W. E. B. DuBois

Martin Luther King Sr. greatly influenced his famous son.

These students are learning important skills at Tuskegee Institute.

King Gets an Education in Segregation

As a boy, one of King's friends was a white boy. This boy's father owned a nearby store. During the school year, King went to the *colored* school and his friend went to the *white* school. (In the early 1900s, people used the word *colored* instead of *black* or *African American*.) Schools for white children had better **facilities** (fuh-SIL-uh-teez). In many of the schools for African American children, there were few desks and books. One day, King was told that he could not be friends with this white boy anymore. This made him very upset. Segregation did not make sense to him.

King attended a school much like this one when he was a child.

Thurgood Marshall

African Americans around the country celebrated *Brown v. Board of Education.*

In 1954, a major segregation law changed. A seven-year-old named Linda Brown lived close to a white's only school. Because she was African American, she had to go to the colored school across town. Her father sued the school system and won. This famous case is called *Brown v. Board of Education of Topeka, Kansas*. From then on, the law stated that schools had to be **desegregated** (dee-SEG-rih-gay-tuhd). Separate was not equal. Many states refused to enforce this law.

An Important Lawyer

Thurgood Marshall was an African American lawyer. He worked for the NAACP.

In the *Brown v. Board of Education* case, Marshall argued that separate could never be equal. He said that having separate schools sent the message that African Americans were not as good as whites. This policy kept the African American students from learning. The Supreme Court agreed and ruled that segregation in schools was **illegal** (il-LEE-guhl). It was a huge victory.

In 1967, President Lyndon Johnson appointed Marshall to the Supreme Court. Marshall was the first African American to serve in this role.

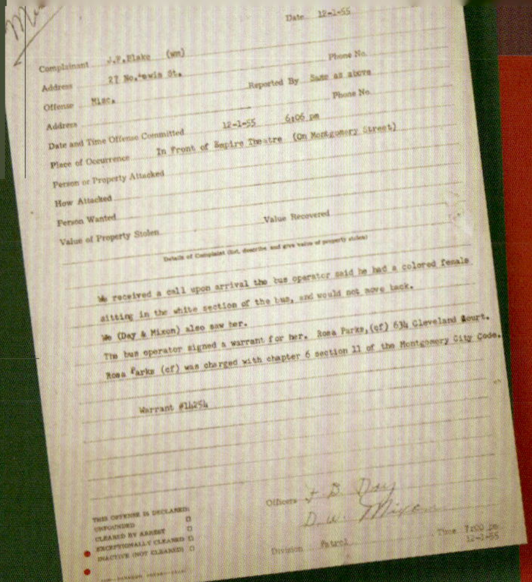
Date 12-1-55
Complainant J.F.Blake (wm) Phone No.
Address 27 No. Lewis St. Reported By Same as above
Offense Misc. Phone No.
Address
Date and Time Offense Committed 12-1-55 6:06 pm
Place of Occurrence In Front of Empire Theatre (On Montgomery Street)
Person or Property Attacked
How Attacked
Person Wanted
Value of Property Stolen Value Recovered
Details of Complaint (list, describe and give value of property stolen)
We received a call upon arrival the bus operator said he had a colored female sitting in the white section of the bus, and would not move back.
We (Day & Mixon) also saw her.
The bus operator signed a warrant for her. Rosa Parks, (cf) 634 Cleveland Court.
Rosa Parks (cf) was charged with chapter 6 section 11 of the Montgomery City Code.
Warrant #14254
Officers F. B. Day
D. W. Mixon
THIS OFFENSE IS DECLARED:
UNFOUNDED
CLEARED BY ARREST
EXCEPTIONALLY CLEARED
INACTIVE (NOT CLEARED)
Division Patrol Time 7:00 pm 12-1-55

Rosa Parks's arrest report

Saying "No"

In 1955, an African American woman named Rosa Parks made a choice. She decided not to give up her seat when the bus she was on filled up. The bus driver told her to move to the back of the bus, but she just sat there quietly. He did not know that Parks was an NAACP activist. The bus driver called the police and had her arrested.

This was not the first time an African American refused to give up a seat on a bus. But this time was different. The African Americans in Montgomery joined together. This type of peaceful protest was new.

Transportation Segregation

Buses in the South had signs that said African Americans could only ride in the back. While in high school, King traveled to a town 90 miles (145 km) away to give a speech. He spoke about African Americans and the Constitution. While traveling home, he had to give up his seat on the bus to a white person.

It was usually the lawyers who fought against segregation. But for real change to take place, everyone needed to stand up against unfair laws. African Americans needed to join together as a community. In this way, they could bring about change.

King was just a young preacher in Montgomery in 1955. On December 1, Rosa Parks refused to give up her seat on a bus. A local civil rights activist, Jo Ann Robinson, helped start a bus **boycott**. King and other leaders gathered at King's church. They decided to make the boycott last more than just one day. King said, "We have no alternative but to protest." He encouraged people to stay off the buses. This made the city officials mad, so they outlawed the boycott. They sent King to jail and fined him $500 for violating this new law. The **media** printed stories in papers and showed King on television. NAACP lawyers fought the case in court. At the same time, Montgomery's African Americans made a difference on the streets. Finally, the Supreme Court ruled that bus segregation was against the law.

Rosa Parks is fingerprinted after being arrested.

Sitting Down to Get the Job Done

On February 1, 1960, four African American college students walked into a Woolworth's department store. They bought school supplies and then sat down at the lunch counter to eat. At that time, however, African Americans could not eat at white-only lunch counters. The young men sat there until the store closed without getting any food. The next day, more African American students returned to the store and sat at the lunch counter. Again, they were not served. This type of protest was called a sit-in. The media soon found out about this story and followed it. It took six months, but the sit-in worked. This lunch counter was desegregated.

This is the second day of the Woolworth's sit-in that took place in Greensboro, North Carolina.

King is arrested after a sit-in. He was arrested 30 times during the Civil Rights Movement.

King liked that these students protested in a peaceful way. Some supporters of King worried that these young activists would make white people mad. This placed King in an awkward position. He felt he had to bridge the gap between the older **generation** and the younger one.

In the end, King felt that the young people were right. Later that year, King participated in a sit-in at the same kind of counter in his town. The police arrested King and others. They were charged with **trespassing**. Sit-ins like this led to the desegregation of lunch counters.

The CORE Leader

James Farmer was the leader of the Congress of Racial Equality (CORE). His group came up with a way to test segregated interstate travel. They organized the Freedom Riders. This was a group of African American and white people. They traveled together on buses, trains, and planes across state lines. They waited in the same waiting rooms and sat together. Some southern states were refusing to follow desegregation laws.

Farmer believed that the Freedom Rides would create a crisis. Then the government would have to step in. He was right. Angry crowds in Alabama attacked these groups. Mobs slashed the buses' tires, beat the riders, and set some of the buses on fire. This got the attention of the government. Desegregation of buses, trains, and planes was finally enforced.

The Battle for Birmingham

Birmingham was a segregated city in Alabama. King knew he had to go there. He planned to protest at department stores. The stores wanted African Americans to shop there. But, African Americans were not allowed to use the stores' restrooms. And, they could not eat at the lunch counters.

King showed up in old clothes. He wanted to show that he would rather wear old work clothes than shop for nice clothes at these stores. He called the plan Project C. The C stood for **confrontation** (kon-fruhn-TAY-shuhn). He hoped to get the store owners to react in a bad way to his peaceful protest. Then, the media would report it. That would bring attention to what was happening.

Many African Americans in Birmingham did not want to get involved. Some were middle-class **citizens**. They did not want to give up what they had worked so hard to achieve. Others knew they would lose their jobs if they joined in the protest. King ended up being arrested. That got the media's attention!

Civil Rights President

It was the Freedom Rides that introduced President John F. Kennedy to the Civil Rights Movement. Newspapers around the world carried pictures of burned-out buses. Kennedy decided to do something about civil rights.

Kennedy started to enforce desegregation laws. At times Kennedy called the governors of southern states and pressured them into controlling the violence. Other times, he sent troops to protect the civil rights workers.

It was the events in Birmingham, Alabama, that made Kennedy realize that the nation needed a civil rights bill. In June 1963, Kennedy proposed a bill that made it illegal to practice segregation. This included lunch counters, jobs, and restrooms. Kennedy's plans gave many African Americans hope that things would change for good. But this bill upset some southerners, and they still refused to obey these laws.

Police officers sometimes used fire hoses to spray protesters.

King is arrested in Birmingham for taking a stand against segregation.

While in jail, King wrote a very famous letter known as the Letter from a Birmingham Jail.

A Letter from Jail

King's time in the Birmingham jail was hard. At first, police placed King all alone in a narrow cell that did not have a mattress. He knew his supporters had run out of bail money. To top it off, eight white ministers in the town wrote a statement for the local paper. In this statement, they urged African Americans to stop protesting.

King felt that he must respond to this statement. He had nothing to write with in jail. So, over a couple of days, his lawyer **smuggled** in a pen and paper. In his response letter, King explained why African Americans had to protest. He said that the only way to spur change was to bring attention to it. Protesting does this. Only then, will people see that change is needed.

His arrest got the attention King wanted. More than 1,000 children and young adults joined together at a church. They held a peaceful meeting. Unfortunately, the police brought in dogs to attack them and fire hoses to spray them. The media caught this on tape, and the nation watched these terrible events in horror. Through peaceful actions, King got the nation's attention focused on the civil rights problems.

Roy Wilkins and Medgar Evers are arrested while peacefully demonstrating. These two men were leaders of the NAACP.

Medgar Evers—Hero

Medgar Evers spent his short life working toward a peaceful **integrated** (IN-tuh-gray-ted) society. When he was young, Evers wanted to register to vote. He was turned away. When he wanted to enter law school, he was turned away because he was African American.

Evers worked for the NAACP in Mississippi. He investigated crimes against African American people. One famous case was the killing of an African American teenager named Emmitt Till. Evers worked to find out who killed Till. He risked his life helping witnesses, who identified the white killers, escape to safety outside of Mississippi.

On June 12, 1963, a white man shot Evers in the back and he died. Evers's death inspired many African Americans to work toward integration. More than 3,000 people attended his funeral. It took more than 30 years to bring Evers's killer to justice.

March on Washington

The nation needed to see that African Americans and whites could stand together in peace. So, African American leaders planned a march. They marched for freedom and for jobs. In 1963, in the heat of summer, 250,000 people gathered in Washington, D.C.

They chose King to deliver the final speech on that August day. King had a speech prepared, but the words were bitter. He felt frustrated having to wait for civil rights. As he spoke, he noticed the crowd was joyful and excited. He put aside his prepared speech and spoke from his heart about his own dreams. His words were very powerful and moving.

It was fitting that he spoke these words in front of Abraham Lincoln's statue. One hundred years earlier, Lincoln had freed the slaves in the South. This day was a powerful moment in American history. This march changed how the nation felt about civil rights. It is still remembered today.

More About Marches

A. Philip Randolph was the editor of a Harlem magazine. He felt that people were powerful. If you get large numbers of people to protest, change will happen. The 1963 march in Washington, D.C., was his idea.

He planned his first march in 1941 to protest racial discrimination. Some companies received money from the government, but they were not fair to African American workers. President Franklin Roosevelt agreed to create a committee that banned racial discrimination in the workplace. In return, Randolph agreed to cancel the march.

These civil rights leaders are promoting the Washington, D.C., march.

Over 250,000 people attended the March on Washington on August 28, 1963.

We Want to Vote!

In the summer of 1964, there were bombings, burnings, and beatings. Segregationists did this because of an event called Freedom Summer. Young people from the North made their way to Mississippi. They hoped to register African American voters. In 1964, Jim Crow laws made African Americans pass tricky tests in order to vote. The questions on these tests were unfair. These summer workers set up schools. At these schools, African Americans were taught important **literacy** skills. This helped them pass the unfair voting tests. If these African Americans could vote, then they could change the policies in their states and towns.

King leads marchers into Mississippi to help African Americans register to vote.

Freedom marchers help this man register to vote.

Although the Civil Rights Act of 1964 gave African Americans the right to vote, some towns still held on to their Jim Crow laws. This was the case in Selma, Alabama. There were 15,000 African Americans who lived there, but fewer than 350 of them had registered to vote. King planned a campaign there hoping that it would force the town to obey the law.

Police beat marchers and poked them with cattle prods. With every march, the jail filled up with African Americans. By this time, King was a **Nobel Peace Prize** winner. Whenever he went to jail, the media paid attention.

A Student and a Marcher

James Meredith became the first African American student to enter the University of Mississippi in 1962. At first, the governor of Mississippi tried to block Meredith from the campus. The federal government had to send in troops to protect Meredith. The white crowd turned violent and gunfire broke out. The campus turned into a battlefield and President Kennedy ordered 16,000 more troops to keep the peace. Meredith stayed on as a student, but his years there were difficult.

Years later, Meredith decided to march against fear. He did this to get people's attention focused on African American rights. He planned to march from Tennessee to Mississippi. On the second day of his march, a white man shot and wounded him. This tragedy caught the attention of King and other leaders. They rushed to the hospital and vowed to finish his march.

The Civil Right's President

President Kennedy was **assassinated** in 1963. Vice President Johnson took over as president. Johnson understood the need for African Americans to have equal rights. Johnson signed the Civil Rights Act of 1964 into law. This law banned segregation in some public locations. However, this law did not protect African Americans from violence or guarantee their right to vote.

During the 1964 campaign, Johnson showed preference to some southern white supporters. Many African Americans felt **betrayed**. But Johnson had to be careful not to offend voters who would give him the nomination. After his election, Johnson looked to King to help him. He went on television and said, "It is wrong—deadly wrong—to deny any of your fellow Americans the right to vote in this country." He helped push through the Voting Rights Act of 1965.

President Johnson signed the Civil Rights Act into law in 1964.

From Selma to Montgomery

In February 1965, a police officer killed an African American man. The young man was trying to protect his family from being beaten. King and others decided to lead a civil rights march to protest this violence. Many people made their way to Selma, Alabama, to join the march. Marchers planned to walk from Selma to the Alabama state capitol building in Montgomery.

As they neared a bridge in Selma, troopers attacked the marchers. Police used clubs and bullwhips. Today, that awful day is called Bloody Sunday. Luckily, the media caught this violence on camera. When the public saw it, they were outraged and planned marches in their own cities. President Lyndon B. Johnson vowed to pass a stricter voting rights bill. This new law banned voting tests and restrictions. Now, African Americans could finally vote. They had more control over who would stay in office.

A young African American woman proudly casts her vote.

King Clashes with Some

There were some African Americans who did not like King's tactics. One of these included a man named Malcolm X. He felt that King's idea of nonviolence left African Americans **vulnerable** (VUHL-nur-uh-buhl). He wanted African Americans to stand up and fight back. Unlike King, Malcolm X wanted the races to stay separate. People who were impatient for change took sides with Malcolm X. His strong stance gave hope and pride to many African Americans.

Other African Americans were against King's tactics, too. One group was called the Black Panther Party for Self-Defense. They carried guns to protect themselves. King tried to convince others that African American **supremacy** was as bad as white supremacy. He felt violence was not the answer to this problem.

Martin Luther King Jr. and Malcolm X meet after a press conference.

Marcus Garvey

About this time, the United States entered the Vietnam Conflict. President Johnson shifted his focus from civil rights to the war. King was upset that Johnson spent billions of dollars on the war. He thought it was more important to help the poor African Americans in the streets of America. When King spoke out against the war, Johnson took it personally.

Hopes for Africa

Marcus Garvey was an African American leader. He led a large **black nationalist** movement in the 1920s. His message was one of pride. He wanted to see African Americans return to Africa.

The Nation of Islam

Malcolm X followed the teachings of the Nation of Islam. This was an African American group in America. Elijah Muhammad (ih-LIE-juh moh-HAH-muhd) was their leader. He taught that white people were evil. He preached that African Americans should form a separate nation. Malcolm X was a powerful speaker. He traveled around the country speaking for the Nation of Islam. In March 1964, Malcolm X left the Nation of Islam. He no longer believed in what Muhammad preached. He was later shot to death by members of the Nation of Islam.

The Black Panthers

The Black Panther Party for Self-Defense was a group who caught the attention of the media. They dressed in black leather jackets, wore **berets** (bur-RAYZ) on their heads, and carried guns. They believed in making their point by causing whites to fear them. This stance did not sit well with King. He taught others that "black power" was just another form of racism.

Watts Riots

Poverty was a serious problem in many cities. Los Angeles was one of them. Laws in California were making it harder to find housing and jobs. In 1965, a white police officer pulled over two young African Americans. As the officer questioned the men, a crowd gathered. A fight broke out and more police officers got involved.

This sparked a riot in the African American community. African Americans who were frustrated came out to the streets and destroyed businesses. To get equal rights, they felt they had to demand it. After six days of riots, the violence ended.

The Black Panther Party (shown above) began in California in 1966.

Thirty-five people were killed and thousands more were injured during the Los Angeles riots.

Poor People's Campaign

King's nonviolent approach did rid the South of Jim Crow laws. But it did not fix all the problems that African Americans faced. King saw that poverty was a big problem. African Americans believed that poor white people lived better than they did. It was easier for white people to find good neighborhoods. They had clean streets and low crime. They could get jobs, too.

King went to Chicago to protest, but what he found shocked him. Both the white mayor and African Americans who lived there opposed King's ideas. The mayor said he was already working to end poverty. King knew the mayor's plan was not working. He also knew he could not get close to the poor unless he lived among them. So in 1966, King moved into the Chicago slums to prove his point. He hoped to convince people to stand up for their rights by using nonviolent means. Still, many people refused to listen to King.

King organized the Chicago Freedom Movement to work for better jobs and higher pay. This group wanted to help the city's poor through nonviolent means.

Marches like this helped bring attention to the problems in American cities.

The Fate of a Nonviolent Man

In 1968, King traveled to Memphis to help workers get better pay. As they marched, some marchers got violent. They broke store windows and caused other damage. King and other leaders had to leave Memphis quickly. King was blamed for the violence. He decided to go back to Memphis and try again. But this time, it would be a peaceful march.

On April 4, 1968, King was at his hotel in Memphis. As he was getting ready to go out to dinner with other civil rights leaders, a white man assassinated him. The news of King's death shook the nation. There were riots in many cities around the United States. King spent his life fighting against violence. And it killed him in the end.

Just days after King's death, Johnson signed another civil rights bill. This bill made it against the law to **discriminate** (dis-KRIM-uh-nate) when selling or renting houses. King's work inspired other nations to seek civil rights laws, too. In the 1990s, segregation in South Africa finally came to an end. King dreamed of the day that his children would "not be judged by the color of their skin, but by the content of their character." King did not see this dream through to completion. But his dream of nonviolence has lived on through today.

Over 50,000 people walked behind King's casket. It was a very peaceful funeral.

Free At Last

These words are engraved on King's tomb in Atlanta, Georgia.

"Free at last. Free at last.
Thank God Almighty
I'm Free at last."

A Supporter of Civil Rights, Too

Coretta Scott King was also a supporter of civil rights. She wanted to march alongside her husband to show that she cared for civil rights, too. But people thought it was too dangerous. Since King was gone much of the time, Mrs. King stayed home to raise their children.

After his death, she marched in Memphis where King was shot. She devoted her life to teaching others about King's ideas of nonviolence. Wherever she went, she was a sign of hope and a reminder of the meaning of the Civil Rights Movement. She continued working for civil rights until her death in 2006.

Glossary

activist—someone who protests and fights for something he or she believes in

assassinated—murdered by surprise attack; usually a prominent person for political reasons

berets—small flat hats

betrayed—to have broken an agreement with someone

black nationalist—a person who believes that African Americans should set up their own social, political, and economic systems separate from white people

boycott—to not buy from or give business to

citizens—people who have the right to live in a country because they were born there or people who have received the legal papers needed to live in a country

confrontation—to have a face to face meeting between people who disagree

desegregated—stopped separation based on race

discriminate—to treat unfairly because of race

facilities—buildings or places where people meet

generation—a group of individuals born around the same time

illegal—against the law

integrated—opened to everyone no matter what race they are

legal—based on laws or rules

literacy—having to do with reading and writing

media—newspapers, radios, and television

Nobel Peace Prize—international awards given out each year; King was presented with the award in 1964.

segregation—forced separation of groups based on race

segregationists—those who want to keep groups separated because of race

smuggled—sneaked; hid from officials

supremacy—better than; to be superior

trespassing—to walk on private property

vulnerable—open to attack

Index

Image Credits

cover The Library of Congress; p.1 The Library of Congress; p.4 The Library of Congress; p.5 The Granger Collection, New York; p.6 (top) The Library of Congress; p.6 (bottom) The Library of Congress; p.7 (top) Hulton Archive/Getty Images; p.7 (bottom) The Library of Congress; p.8 Corbis; p.9 (left) Bettmann/Corbis; p.9 (right) The Library of Congress; p.10 The National Archives; p.11 The Granger Collection, New York; p.12 Bettmann/Corbis; p.13 (left) Flip Schulke/Corbis; p.13 (right) The Library of Congress; p.15 (top) Bettmann/Corbis; p.15 (bottom) The Library of Congress; p.16 Bettmann/Corbis; p.17 Bettmann/Corbis; p.19 (top) The Library of Congress; p.19 (bottom) The Library of Congress; p.20 Bettmann/Corbis; p.21 Bettmann/Corbis; p.22 The Library of Congress; p.23 The Library of Congress; p.24 The Library of Congress; p.25 The Library of Congress; p.26 (top) David Fenton/Hulton Archive/Getty Images; p.26 (bottom) Hulton Archive/Getty Images; p.27 The Library of Congress; p.29 Lynn Pelham/Time Life Pictures/Getty Images